PRAYING

The

Old Testament

Compiled by
Philip Law

from the words of
THE GOOD NEWS BIBLE

Introduction by Richard Holloway
Bishop of Edinburgh

TRI∧NGLE

First published 1989
Triangle
SPCK
Holy Trinity Church
Marylebone Road
London NW1 4DU

British Library Cataloguing in Publication Data

Law, Philip, *1958–*
    Praying with the Old Testament.
    1. Christian life. Prayers – Devotional works
    I. Title
    242'.8

    ISBN 0-281-04407-4

Typeset by Rowland Phototypesetting Ltd
Bury St Edmunds, Suffolk
Printed in Great Britain by
Hazell, Watson and Viney Ltd
Member of BPCC
Aylesbury, Bucks.

Contents

An asterisk (*) following the Bible reference after a prayer indicates that the Bible text has been adapted or expanded.

Introduction

Joan is the mother of several young children, and she thinks she's on the verge of a nervous breakdown. Her children are energetic and quarrelsome, and she's appalled at her lack of patience with them, her sudden gusts of anger. She's resentful of her husband, who's rarely at home and likes a quiet life when he is. Recently, she's had one minor illness after another: pains and headaches and general listlessness. Right now she's depressed, constantly on the brink of tears.

William is her husband. He is in the middle of a demanding career, and he's terribly overworked. He enjoys his work, but he's moody and discontented at home and finds his wife increasingly irritable and uncongenial. Somehow he feels he's lost direction, that something has gone out of his life. He finds himself casting sidelong and wistful glances at the young women he works with. The future beckons him with little real joy.

Agnes is old and lives alone. All her relatives and most of her friends are dead. She's anxious about what will happen to her when she can't look after herself. The future scares her.

John is single, in his middle thirties. He seems unable to establish any kind of long-lasting relationship. He's worried by an increasing intolerance in his attitudes towards others, though he does little to offset it. Most of his life now is spent pursuing his own interests and pleasures. He's not sure that he likes what he's turning into, but he cannot summon up the energy or the wisdom to alter the prospect.

All go to the same church. More unconsciously than consciously, they are aware of a large gap between the quality of their lives and the claims made by their faith. Sometimes they're not sure if they really believe, anyway. Surely, if they really believed it would make more difference in and to their lives? On the other hand, since they are honest people, they will admit they've never worked very hard at it. They feel a bit guilty because they never pray, except sometimes in church, if they get there before the service begins – a rare enough occurrence. Occasionally the Vicar preaches about prayer – rather uncomfortably it has to be admitted, but he's not a conspicuous example of serenity, anyway, and they never really feel moved to make an effort. At bottom they feel they are on their own in life and must muddle through as best they can. There are no magical deliverances. Even so, sometimes they all wish they could discover something that would change them, help them to cope, or be better or nicer. But none of them really has much hope that they will ever find it.

That is a picture of stress, and churning, purposeless dissatisfaction. Though Joan and William and Agnes and John are fictitious, the situations they represent are true enough. Like Martha in the story told by St Luke, they are troubled and anxious about many things. They come to church half hoping to find an answer, but never really hearing it.

Well then, is there any answer? Can anything be done? That depends: it depends upon whether or not we *are* on our own in life. And I'm not talking about friends: they are very important: they'll listen to us and support us when we need it, but that only soothes, it doesn't heal, it doesn't alter our predicament. The question is: is there really, as the Church claims, and as the Bible writers believed, a power in the universe which we can lay hold of, gradually and increasingly, which will mend us and heal us, give us the strength to endure? More, will that presence give us joy, bring a savour back into existence?

The galling thing here is that we never get an answer to that question in advance of our own experience. We are not given a clear and convincing proof which then motivates us to trust it. We are invited, instead, to live by faith. We are not given the answer all at once, and once for all. We have to live experimentally, bit by bit, trusting that if we follow a certain way, certain things will, in time, happen. We prove the power and the presence by living as though it were there: and that activity is called prayer. Prayer is faith in action. Prayer is experimental faith. Prayer, as believers have experienced it down the centuries, is the systematic activity of opening our life, our consciousness, to that power we long to lay hold of. Obviously, it isn't going to be easy, though it really isn't all that hard. Our minds are full of our own anxieties and concerns, that great jumble of distractions and memories which floats about inside us. A large part of prayer is simply concerned with learning to turn all that off so that we can pay increasing attention to that other presence which is also within us, so that it can gradually invade us, and gently control us. And all that can only be done by doing it.

Time is all we need to find, and a lot of what we do in praying is valid even if we don't fully believe in God. Many people who are not believers practise a form of meditation, because the practice itself is beneficial. There is even an increasing scientific interest in the fact. It is possible to wire people up and monitor their brainwaves when they are meditating. It has been conclusively demonstrated that real and measurable alterations take place, not only in the interior consciousness, but within the very organism. This, however, is the negative part of prayer: an exercise that removes stress and tension when systematically practised, when we have learned to turn the conscious mind off and simply rest in another form of consciousness. There are two steps in this process.

First of all, there is the achieving of stillness, physical stillness: assuming an erect but relaxed posture, we breathe ourselves into a state of rest and relaxation.

One way to do this is simply to observe ourselves as we breathe: concentrate on the breathing, observe the breath, the breathing in, the holding gently, the breathing out – over and over, till a stillness pervades us.

Next, is the practice of attention or gentle concentration. What is being attempted here is simple: our minds are usually a bewildering kaleidoscope of conflicting thoughts and images and memories. What we need to do, therefore, is to find a way that will tune out all this background static and sharpen the mind to a point, so that we can place our attention on one thing. The ancient technique for this is repetition of a single word or phrase. The Orthodox Church has a whole classical tradition of prayer that is built on the simple repetition of the name of Jesus, so that it resonates through our whole being and becomes part of us. The section 'Old Testament Words for Contemplation', at the end of this book, suggests short Bible phrases which can be used in this way.

But we are not just interested in clearing out the clutter: we want something positive to fill our consciousness, we want to open our minds to the Divine Presence within. Here again, the technique is simple and psychologically straightforward. Jesus said we were to abide in him, grow deeply into him, and let his words abide in us. Today we know a great deal about how our conscious and unconscious minds work, and what we know strongly confirms our Lord's injunction to let his words abide in us, form themselves in us, become part of our minds. We know how people can have their attitudes altered today, have their brains washed by insidious propagandists. Many modern advertising and communication techniques operate on this principle and they form appetites, needs and attitudes within us, although we are often completely oblivious to the process. In a more straightforward way, our minds and opinions are being constantly bombarded by messages from newspapers, radio and television, forming a mind in us, building up a great reservoir of values and convictions, many of them highly dubious. Ours is a loud and overstimulated culture in which the whisper of God is hard to hear.

The practice of systematic prayer is an attempt to give God access to the air-waves of our conscious and unconscious mind, so that his values and something of his nature can be formed in us. And repetition of the great prayers of Scripture, over and over again until they become part of our own nature and pray themselves within us, is a fundamental part of that ancient method. There are in the Scriptures, if we know where to find them, words to help our prayers in every kind of human situation.

The people of the Old Testament were eloquent and passionate in their address to God. At times their calling on God bordered on rudeness in its need:

O Lord, how long must I call for help
    before you listen? . . . (Habbakuk 1.2)[1]

Where is your great concern for us?
Where is your power?
Where are your love and compassion?
Do not ignore us.   (Isaiah 63.15)[2]

But in addition to this robustness, this attack upon God, there are countless prayers of tenderness and longing, particularly in the Psalms:

My whole being desires you;
like a dry, worn-out, and waterless land,
my soul is thirsty for you.   (Psalm 63.1)[3]

Indeed, the Psalter has been called the Prayer Book of the Church. It is probably the greatest resource book of Christian prayer, and we know how Jesus used it to the end of his life and was praying from it on the cross.

[1]See p. 9   [2]See p. 58   [3]See p. 38

xi

His great cry, 'My God, my God, why have you abandoned me?' is a direct quotation from Psalm 22.

But Jesus also knew the other books in the Old Testament, quoted from them and almost certainly used them in his periods of prayer to the Father, when he withdrew from the multitude to be silent and alone. When we pray the prayers of the Old Testament, therefore, we can be certain we are praying the prayers Jesus used. When we repeat them over and over, allowing them to form in our minds, we can be certain that the mind of Jesus is being formed within us. And when we commit ourselves to the risk of prayer, we can be certain that God will meet us and, however unconsciously, that his strength and compassion will support and increasingly strengthen us as we make our way along the path of life.

Richard Holloway

The Lord is in his holy Temple;
let everyone on earth
be silent in his presence

Habakkuk 2.20

My Temple will be called a house of prayer
for the people of all nations

Isaiah 56.7

PERSONAL PRAYERS

WHY, O LORD?

Prayers of doubt and distress

Remember, O God,
my life is only a breath
Job 7.7

Why am I so sad?

As a deer longs for a stream of cool water,
    so I long for you, O God.
I thirst for you, the living God;
    when can I go and worship in your presence?
Day and night I cry,
    and tears are my only food.
Why am I so sad?
    Why am I so troubled?
I will put my hope in God,
    and once again I will praise him,
    my saviour and my God.

Psalm 42.1–3,5

Why have you abandoned me?

My God, my God, why have you
    abandoned me?
I have cried desperately for help,
   but still it does not come.
During the day I call to you, my God,
   but you do not answer;
I call at night,
   but get no rest.

It was you who brought me safely
    through birth,
   and when I was a baby, you kept me safe.
I have relied on you since the day I was born,
   and you have always been my God.
Do not stay away from me!
   Trouble is near,
   and there is no one to help.

Psalm 22.1–2, 9–11

How long, O Lord?

Lord, don't be angry and rebuke me!
  Don't punish me in your anger!
I am worn out, O Lord; have pity on me!
  Give me strength; I am completely exhausted
  and my whole being is deeply troubled.
How long, O Lord, will you wait to help me?

Come and save me, Lord;
  in your mercy rescue me from death.
In the world of the dead you are not remembered;
  no one can praise you there.

Psalm 6.1–5

How much longer?

How much longer will you forget me, Lord?
  For ever?
  How much longer will you hide yourself
    from me?
How long must I endure trouble?
  How long will sorrow fill my heart
    day and night?
How long will my enemies triumph over me?

Look at me, O Lord my God, and answer me.
  Restore my strength; don't let me die.
Don't let my enemies say, 'We have
    defeated him.'
  Don't let them gloat over my downfall.

I rely on your constant love;
  I will be glad, because you will rescue me.
I will sing to you, O Lord,
  because you have been good to me.

Psalm 13.1–6

Why, O Lord?

Why, O Lord, are wicked men so prosperous?
  Why do dishonest men succeed?
You plant them, and they take root;
  they grow and bear fruit,
They always speak well of you,
  yet they do not really care about you.
But, Lord, you know me;
  you see what I do, and how I love you.

Jeremiah 12.1–3*

Why are you silent?

O Lord, how long must I call for help
  before you listen, before you save us from violence?
Why do you make me see such trouble?
How can you endure to look on such wrongdoing?
Destruction and violence are all around me,
  and justice is never done.
Evil men get the better of the righteous,
  and so justice is perverted.
O Lord, you are my God, holy and eternal.
Your eyes are too holy to look at evil.
O Lord, why are you silent?

Habakkuk 1.2–4,12,13*

Why do you avoid me?

Speak first, O God, and I will answer.
    Or let me speak, and you answer me.
What are my sins? What wrongs have I done?
    What crimes am I charged with?
Why do you avoid me?
    Why do you treat me like an enemy?
Are you trying to frighten me? I'm nothing
        but a leaf;
    you are attacking a piece of dry straw.
You bring bitter charges against me,
    even for what I did when I was young.
You bind chains on my feet;
    you watch every step I take, and even
        examine my footprints.
As a result, I crumble like rotten wood,
    like a moth-eaten coat.

Job 13.22–8

Will you even look at me?

We are all born weak and helpless.
    All lead the same short, troubled life.
We grow and wither as quickly as flowers;
    we disappear like shadows.
Will you even look at me, God,
    or put me on trial and judge me?
Nothing clean can ever come
    from anything as unclean as man.
The length of his life is decided beforehand –
    the number of months he will live.
You have settled it, and it can't be changed.

But I will wait for better times,
    wait till this time of trouble is ended.
Then you will call and I will answer,
    and you will be pleased with me, your creature.
Then you will watch every step I take,
    but you will not keep track of my sins.
You will forgive them and put them away;
    you will wipe out all the wrongs I have done.

Job 14.1–5,14–17

BE MERCIFUL, O GOD

Prayers of penitence

I spoke foolishly, Lord
Job 40.3

Lord of Compassion

Lord of Compassion,
You loved me; you called to me
   as a mother calls to her child.
But the more you called to me,
   the more I turned away.
Yet you were the one who taught me to walk;
   you took me up in your arms.
But I did not acknowledge that you
   took care of me.
You drew me to you; you picked me up,
   and held me to your cheek.
You bent down to me and fed me.
Lord of Compassion,
Do not give me up; do not abandon me.
   Do not punish me in your anger!

Hosea 11.1–4,8,9*

I was unfaithful

Almighty Lord,
I was afraid.
Like an unfaithful wife,
like a widow;
desperately lonely.

Call me back to you, Lord.
Do not leave me.
In your deep love,
take me back.
In your anger,
do not turn away.

Isaiah 54.4,6,7,8*

Be merciful, O God

Be merciful to me, O God,
  because of your constant love.
Because of your great mercy
  wipe away my sins!
Wash away all my evil
  and make me clean from my sin!

I recognise my faults;
  I am always conscious of my sins.
I have sinned against you – only against you –
  and done what you consider evil.
So you are right in judging me;
  you are justified in condemning me.
I have been evil from the time I was born;
  from the day of my birth I have been sinful.

Sincerity and truth are what you require;
  fill my mind with your wisdom.
Remove my sin, and I will be clean;
  wash me, and I will be whiter than snow.
Let me hear the sounds of joy and gladness;
  and though you have crushed me and broken me,
  I will be happy once again.
Close your eyes to my sins
  and wipe out all my evil.

Create a pure heart in me, O God,
  and put a new and loyal spirit in me.
Do not banish me from your presence;
  do not take your holy spirit away from me.
Give me again the joy that comes from your salvation,
  and make me willing to obey you.

Psalm 51.1–12

Hear my cry

From the depths of my despair
   I call to you, Lord.
Hear my cry, O Lord;
   listen to my call for help!
If you kept a record of our sins,
   who could escape being condemned?
But you forgive us,
   so that we should stand in awe of you.

Psalm 130.1–4

Arrow Prayers

Please forgive me, Lord.
I have no right to say anything.

Genesis 18.27*

Please don't be angry, Lord.

Genesis 18.30

Lord, I am not worth all the kindness and
faithfulness that you have shown me.

Genesis 32.10

Lord, I have committed a terrible sin!
Please forgive me.
I have acted foolishly.

2 Samuel 24.10*

Look, O Lord, at my agony,
at the anguish of my soul!
My heart is broken in sorrow for my sins.

Lamentations 1.20

YOU ARE WITH ME

Faith in God's blessings

God bless you
Genesis 43.29

Listen to my prayer

Lord my God,
I am your servant.
Listen to my prayer,
and grant the requests
I make to you today.

1 Kings 8.28

You are with me

Lord my God,
Let me not be afraid
or discouraged;
for I know you are with me
wherever I go.

Joshua 1.9*

Praise it is most Holy name !!!

Lord, heal me

Lord, I will live for you, for you alone;
heal me and let me live.
My bitterness will turn into peace.
You save my life from all danger;
you forgive all my sins.
No one in the world of the dead can
    praise you;
The dead cannot trust in your faithfulness.
It is the living who praise you,
as I praise you now.

Isaiah 38.16–19

I have tried

Remember, Lord, that I have served you
    faithfully and loyally,
And that I have always tried to do
    what you wanted me to.

2 Kings 20.3

You are king

I will proclaim your greatness,
    my God and king;
  I will thank you for ever and ever.
Every day I will thank you;
  I will praise you for ever and ever.
The Lord is great and is to be highly praised;
  his greatness is beyond understanding.
The Lord is loving and merciful,
  slow to become angry and full of constant love.
He is good to everyone
  and has compassion on all he made.

All your creatures, Lord, will praise you,
  and all your people will give you thanks.
They will speak of the glory of your
      royal power
  and tell of your might,
so that everyone will know your mighty deeds
  and the glorious majesty of your kingdom.
Your rule is eternal,
  and you are king for ever.

Psalm 145.1–3,8–13

22

You are my saviour

I praise you, Lord!
You were angry with me,
  but now you comfort me and are angry no longer.
You are my saviour;
  I will trust in you and not be afraid.
You give me power and strength;
  you are my saviour.
As fresh water brings joy to the thirsty,
  so your people rejoice when you save them.

Isaiah 12.1–3*

You give shelter

Lord, you are my God;
   I will honour you and praise your name.
The people of powerful nations will praise you;
   you will be feared in the cities of cruel nations.
The poor and the helpless have fled to you
   and have been safe in times of trouble.
You give them shelter from storms
   and shade from the burning heat.
Cruel men attack like a winter storm,
   like drought in a dry land.
But you, Lord, you silence the shouts of cruel men,
   as a cloud cools a hot day.

Isaiah 25.1,3–5

You strengthen

Lord, why do I complain that you do not
    know my troubles
  or care if I suffer injustice?
You are the everlasting God;
  you created all the world.
You never grow tired or weary,
  and no one understands your thoughts.
Yet you strengthen those who are weak
    and tired.
Those who trust in you for help
  will find their strength renewed.

*Isaiah 40.27,28,29,31**

You have helped me!

You, O Lord, have filled my heart with joy;
　　how happy I am because of what you
　　　　have done!
I laugh at my enemies;
　　how joyful I am because you have
　　　　helped me!

No one is holy like the Lord;
　　there is none like him,
　　no protector like our God.
Stop your loud boasting;
　　silence your proud words.
For the Lord is a God who knows,
　　and he judges all that people do.
The bows of strong soldiers are broken,
　　but the weak grow strong.
The people who once were well fed
　　now hire themselves out to get food,
　　but the hungry are hungry no more.
The childless wife has borne seven children,
　　but the mother of many is left with none.
The Lord kills and restores to life;
　　he sends people to the world of the dead
　　and brings them back again.
He makes some men poor and others rich;
　　he humbles some and makes others great.
He lifts the poor from the dust
　　and raises the needy from their misery.
He makes them companions of princes
　　and puts them in places of honour.

You, O Lord, have filled my heart with joy;
   how happy I am because of what you
      have done!
I laugh at my enemies;
   how joyful I am because you have
      helped me!

1 Samuel 2.1–8*

You answered me

From the bottom of the pit, O Lord,
   I cried out to you.
When I begged you to listen to my cry,
   you heard.
You answered me and told me not to be afraid.

Lamentations 3.55–7

The Lord bless you!

May the Lord bless you
   and take care of you;
May the Lord be kind and gracious to you;
May the Lord look on you with favour
   and give you peace.

Numbers 6.24–6

Arrow Blessings

The Lord be with you!

Ruth 2.4

The Lord bless you!

Ruth 2.4

May the Lord reward you
for what you have done.

Ruth 2.12

Arrow Prayers

Lord, give me success today.

Genesis 24.12*

Almighty Lord, look at me, your servant!
See my trouble and remember me!

1 Samuel 1.11

You, Lord, are my light;
you dispel my darkness.

2 Samuel 22.29

Bless me, God.
Be with me and keep me from anything evil
that might cause me pain.

1 Chronicles 4.10*

God, make me strong!

Nehemiah 6.9

Remember me, O God, and spare me
because of your great love.

Nehemiah 13.22

Almighty Lord, you are a just judge;
I have placed my cause in your hands.

Jeremiah 11.20

Lord, you are the one who protects me
and gives me strength;
you help me in times of trouble.

Jeremiah 16.19

Lord, heal me and I will be completely well;
rescue me and I will be perfectly safe.
You are the one I praise!

Jeremiah 17.14

O, Lord, I prayed to you,
and in your holy Temple you heard me.
Salvation comes from the Lord!

Jonah 2.7,9

SHOW ME THE WAY

Delight in God's law

My God, let me serve you
with an undivided heart
and a willing mind
1 Chronicles 28.9*

You alone

O Lord my God,
You alone will I worship.
Nothing else in heaven or earth
can take your place.

Deuteronomy 5.6–8

With all my heart

O Lord my God,
Give me the will to obey
    your commandments,
to be faithful to you,
    and serve you
with all my heart and soul.

Joshua 22.5*

Teach me your laws

Teach me, Lord, the meaning of your laws,
    and I will obey them at all times.
Explain your law to me, and I will obey it;
    I will keep it with all my heart.
Keep me obedient to your commandments,
    because in them I find happiness.
Give me the desire to obey your laws
    rather than to get rich.
Keep me from paying attention to
      what is worthless;
    be good to me, as you have promised.
Enable me to speak the truth at all times,
    because my hope is in your judgements.
I will always obey your law,
    for ever and ever.
I will live in perfect freedom,
    because I try to obey your teachings.

Psalm 119.33–7,43–5

Give me wisdom

Dear Father,
May your spirit give me wisdom
that I may know your will,
that I may honour you,
and find pleasure in obeying you.

Isaiah 11.2,3*

Show me the way

Dear Lord, I trust in you with all my heart.
Let me not rely on what I think I know,
but help me to remember you in everything I do.

Dear Lord, show me the right way.
Let me not think that I am wiser than I am,
but help me to obey you and refuse to do wrong.

Proverbs 3.5–6*

Help me do good

Whenever I possibly can, O Lord,
help me do good to those who need it.
And never let me tell my neighbour
  to wait until tomorrow
  if I can help him now.

*Proverbs 3.27–8**

Keep me from lying

I ask you, God, to let me have two things
  before I die:
keep me from lying,
and let me neither be rich nor poor.

Proverbs 30.7

God of all Wisdom

God of all Wisdom,
Help me to think before I speak,
before I make rash promises.
For you are in heaven and I am on earth,
so I will say no more than I have to.
Help me to realise that the more I talk,
the more likely I am to say something foolish.
So when I make a promise to you, O my God,
help me keep it as quickly as possible!

Ecclesiastes 5.2–4*

MY HEART IS QUIET

Joy in God's presence

*Let me see
the dazzling light of your presence.*
Exodus 33.18

O God, you are my God

O God, you are my God, and I long for you.
  My whole being desires you;
like a dry, worn-out, and waterless land,
  my soul is thirsty for you.

O God, you are my God

Let me see you in the sanctuary;
  let me see how mighty and glorious you are.
Your constant love is better than life itself,
  and so I will praise you.

O God, you are my God

I will give you thanks as long as I live;
  I will raise my hands to you in prayer.
My soul will feast and be satisfied,
  and I will sing glad songs of praise to you.

O God, you are my God

Psalm 63.1–5*

My God, my love

Come to me, my God, my love;
   my darling Lord, come to me.
The winter is over; the rains have stopped;
   in the countryside the flowers are in bloom.
This is the time for singing;
   the song of doves is heard in the fields.
Figs are beginning to ripen;
   the air is fragrant with blossoming vines.
Come to me, then, my God, my love;
   my darling Lord, come to me.
You are like a dove that hides
   in the crevice of a rock.
Let me see your lovely face
   and hear your enchanting voice.

Song of Songs 2.10–14*

My shepherd

The Lord is my shepherd;
   I have everything I need.
He lets me rest in fields of green grass
   and leads me to quiet pools of fresh water.
He gives me new strength.
He guides me in the right paths,
   as he has promised.
Even if I go through the deepest darkness,
   I will not be afraid, Lord,
      for you are with me.
Your shepherd's rod and staff protect me.

You prepare a banquet for me,
   where all my enemies can see me;
you welcome me as an honoured guest
   and fill my cup to the brim.
I know that your goodness and love will be
   with me all my life;
      and your house will be my home as long
      as I live.

Psalm 23

Surrounded with joy

Sing praise to the Lord,
    all his faithful people!
Remember what the Holy One has done,
    and give him thanks!
His anger lasts only a moment,
    his goodness for a lifetime.
Tears may flow in the night,
    but joy comes in the morning.

I felt secure and said to myself,
    'I will never be defeated.'
You were good to me, Lord;
    you protected me like a mountain fortress.
But then you hid yourself from me,
    and I was afraid.

I called to you, Lord;
    I begged for your help;
'What will you gain from my death?
    What profit from my going to the grave?
Are dead people able to praise you?
    Can they proclaim your unfailing goodness?
Hear me, Lord, and be merciful!
    Help me, Lord!'

You have changed my sadness into
    a joyful dance;
    you have taken away my sorrow
    and surrounded me with joy.
So I will not be silent;
    I will sing praise to you.
Lord, you are my God,
    I will give you thanks for ever.

Psalm 30.4–12

Where could I escape?

Lord, you have examined me
  and you know me.
You know everything I do;
  from far away you understand all my thoughts.
You see me, whether I am working or resting;
  you know all my actions.
Even before I speak,
  you already know what I will say.
You are all round me on every side;
  you protect me with your power.
Your knowledge of me is too deep;
  it is beyond my understanding.

Where could I go to escape from you?
  Where could I get away from your presence?
If I went up to heaven, you would be there;
  if I lay down in the world of the dead,
    you would be there.
If I flew away beyond the east
  or lived in the farthest place in the west,
you would be there to lead me,
  you would be there to help me.
I could ask the darkness to hide me
  or the light round me to turn into night,
but even the darkness is not dark for you,
  and the night is as bright as the day.
  Darkness and light are the same to you.

You created every part of me;
  you put me together in my mother's womb.
I praise you because you are to be feared;
  all you do is strange and wonderful.
  I know it with all my heart.

When my bones were being formed,
   carefully put together in my mother's womb,
when I was growing there in secret,
   you knew that I was there –
   you saw me before I was born.
The days allotted to me
   had all been recorded in your book,
   before any of them ever began.
O God, how difficult I find your thoughts;
   how many of them there are!
If I counted them, they would be more than
      the grains of the sand.
   When I awake, I am still with you.

Psalm 139.1–18

My heart is quiet

Lord, I have given up my pride
   and turned away from my arrogance.
I am not concerned with great matters
   or with subjects too difficult for me.
Instead, I am content and at peace.
As a child lies quietly in its mother's arms,
   so my heart is quiet within me.

Psalm 131.1–2

Joy for ever

You, Lord, are all I have,
   and you give me all I need;
   my future is in your hands.
How wonderful are your gifts to me;
   how good they are!

I praise the Lord, because he guides me,
   and in the night my conscience warns me.
I am always aware of the Lord's presence;
   he is near, and nothing can shake me.

And so I am thankful and glad,
   and I feel completely secure,
because you protect me from the
     power of death,
   and the one you love you will not
     abandon to the world of the dead.

You will show me the path that leads to life;
   your presence fills me with joy
   and brings me pleasure for ever.

Psalm 16.5–11

PRAYERS FOR
GROUP WORSHIP

WE ARE FILLED WITH AWE

Humility and hope

Lord God of Heaven!
You are great,
and we stand in fear of you
Nehemiah 1.5

How great you are!

You, Lord, you alone are Lord;
  You made the heavens and the stars of the sky.
You made the land and sea and everything in them;
  you gave life to all.
O God, our God, how great you are!
  How terrifying, how powerful!

Nehemiah 9.6,32

You are king for ever

Remember, O Lord, what has happened to us.
  Look at us, and see our disgrace.
Happiness has gone out of our lives;
  grief has taken the place of our dances.
We are sick at our very hearts
  and can hardly see through our tears.
But you, O Lord, are king for ever,
  and will rule to the end of time.
Bring us back to you, Lord, bring us back!
  Or have you rejected us for ever?

Lamentations 5.1,15,17,19,21,22

We bow our heads before you

O Lord, you have always been our home.
Before you created the hills
   or brought the world into being,
     you were eternally God,
     and will be God for ever.

We bow our heads before you

You tell man to return to what he was;
   you change him back to dust.
A thousand years to you are like one day;
   they are like yesterday, already gone,
   like a short hour in the night.

We bow our heads before you

You carry us away like a flood;
   we last no longer than a dream.
We are like weeds that sprout in the morning,
   that grow and burst into bloom,
   then dry up and die in the evening.

We bow our heads before you

We are destroyed by your anger;
   we are terrified by your fury.
You place our sins before you,
   our secret sins where you can see them.

We bow our heads before you

Our life is cut short by your anger;
   it fades away like a whisper.
Seventy years is all we have –

eighty years, if we are strong;
yet all they bring us is trouble and sorrow;
  life is soon over, and we are gone.

We bow our heads before you

Who has felt the full power of your anger?
  Who knows what fear your fury can bring?
Teach us how short our life is,
  so that we may become wise.

We bow our heads before you

Psalm 90.1–12*

You alone know

O Lord, listen in heaven and judge your servants.
Punish the guilty one as he deserves,
  and acquit the one who is innocent.
You alone know the thoughts of the human heart.
Deal with each person as he deserves,
  so that your people may obey you.

1 Kings 8.32,39,40

We were born with nothing

We were born with nothing,
and we will die with nothing.
You gave, O Lord,
and now you have taken away.
May your name be praised!

Job 1.21*

We are filled with awe

O Lord, we have heard of what you have done.
and we are filled with awe.
Now do again in our times
the great deeds you used to do.
Be merciful, even when you are angry.

Habakkuk 3.2*

Bring us back

Lord, we were like an untamed animal,
    but you taught us to obey.
Bring us back;
    we are ready to return to you,
    the Lord our God.

Jeremiah 31.18

Protect us and save us

Lord, have mercy on us.
    We have put our hope in you.
Protect us day by day
    and save us in times of trouble.

Isaiah 33.2

Heal us and help us

High and holy God,
who lives for ever,
who lives in a high and holy place,
but who also lives with us
if we are humble and repentant:
restore our confidence and hope,
give us life
and do not continue to accuse us;
do not be angry with us for ever.

You were angry with us
because of our sin and greed,
because we were stubborn
and kept going our own way;
but now you heal us and help us,
you comfort those who mourn,
you offer peace to all,
both near and far!

Isaiah 57.15–19*

DO NOT ABANDON US

Prayers for forgiveness

We have sinned
Judges 10.15

How can we live?

We are burdened with sins
and the wrongs we have done.
We are wasting away.
How can we live?

Ezekiel 33.10

We confess

O, God, we are too ashamed
    to raise our heads in your presence.
Our sins pile up, high above our heads;
they reach as high as the heavens.
We confess our guilt to you;
We have no right to come into your presence.

Ezra 9.6,15*

Will you forgive us?

We have sinned and rebelled,
and will you, O God, forgive us?
Or will you pursue us and kill us?
Will your mercy be hidden by your anger,
by a cloud of fury too thick for our prayers
    to get through?

Lamentations 3.42–4*

Lord, look upon us, and forgive

Lord, look upon us from heaven,
where you live in your holiness and glory.
Where is your great concern for us?
Where is your power?
Where are your love and compassion?
Do not ignore us.

Lord, look upon us, and forgive

You are our father, the one who has always
    rescued us.
Why do you let us stray from your ways?
Why do you make us so stubborn that we turn
        away from you?
Come back, for the sake of those who serve you,
for the sake of the people who have
    always been yours.

Lord, look upon us, and forgive

You welcome those who find joy in doing
    what is right,
those who remember how you want them to live.
You were angry with us, but we went on sinning;
in spite of your great anger we have continued
    to do wrong since ancient times.

Lord, look upon us, and forgive

All of us have been sinful;
even our best actions are filthy
    through and through.
Because of our sins we are like leaves that
    wither and are blown away by the wind.
No one turns to you in prayer;
no one goes to you for help.
You have hidden yourself from us and
    abandoned us
    because of our sins.

Lord, look upon us, and forgive

But you are our father, Lord.
We are like clay, and you are the potter.
You created us, so do not be too angry with us
    or hold our sins against us for ever.
We are your people;
be merciful to us.

Lord, look upon us, and forgive

Isaiah 63.15,16,17;64.5–9*

Lord God, we have sinned

Lord God, we have sinned.
We have been evil.
We have done wrong.
We have rejected what you commanded us to do
   and turned away from what you showed us was right.

Lord God, we have sinned

You, Lord, always do what is right,
   but we have always brought disgrace on ourselves.
You are merciful and forgiving,
   although we have rebelled against you.

Lord God, we have sinned

We did not listen to you, O Lord our God.
Even now, we have not tried to please you
   by turning from our sins or by following the truth.

Lord God, we have sinned

Listen to us, O God.
Look at us, and see the trouble we are in.
We are praying to you because you are merciful,
   not because we have done right.

Lord God, we have sinned

Lord, hear us.
Lord, forgive us.
Lord, listen to us, and act!

Daniel 9.4,5,7,9,10,13,18,19*

In your goodness

O Lord, in your goodness
forgive those who are worshipping you
with all their heart,
even though they are not clean.

2 Chronicles 30.19*

Do not abandon us

Even though our sins accuse us,
    help us, Lord, as you have promised.
We have turned away from you many times;
    we have sinned against you.
Why are you like a stranger,
    like a traveller who stays for only one night?
Why are you like a man taken by surprise,
    like a soldier powerless to help?
Surely, Lord, you are with us!
    We are your people; do not abandon us.

Jeremiah 14.7–9

Show us your mercy

Forgive all our sins, O Lord.
Accept our prayer, and we will praise you
    as we have promised.
Show us your mercy, O Lord.
We have no one else to turn to.

*Hosea 14.2,3**

Trample our sins!

There is no other god like you, O Lord;
    you forgive the sins of your people.
You do not stay angry for ever,
    but you take pleasure in showing us
        your constant love.
Be merciful to us once again.
Trample our sins underfoot and send them
    to the bottom of the sea!

*Micah 7.18–19**

Arrow Prayers

Have pity on your people, Lord.

Joel 2.17

Sovereign Lord, forgive your people!

Amos 7.2

ALL THAT WE DESIRE

Trust in God's love

Be a shepherd to your people, Lord
Micah 7.14

In you, O God, we trust

Lord, your constant love reaches the heavens;
   your faithfulness extends to the skies.

In you, O God, we trust

Your righteousness is towering like the mountains;
   your justice is like the depths of the sea.

In you, O God, we trust

How precious, O God, is your constant love!
   We find protection under the shadow of your wings.

In you, O God, we trust

We feast on the abundant food you provide;
   you let us drink from the river of your goodness.

In you, O God, we trust

You are the source of all life,
   and because of your light we see the light.

In you, O God, we trust

Psalm 36.5–9*

Great is your love

Lord of Mercy, slow to become angry
   and full of constant love:
   you do not punish us as we deserve.
As high as the sky is above the earth,
   so great is your love for those who honour you.
As far as the east is from the west,
   so far do you remove our sins from us.
As kind as a father is to his children,
   so kind are you to those who honour you.
For you know, O Lord, what we are made of;
   you remember that we are dust.

*Psalm 103.8,10–14**

Remember our prayers

Lord our God, be with us;
never leave us or abandon us;
make us obedient to you,
that we may always live as you want us to live,
and keep all your laws and commands.
Lord our God, remember at all times
    our prayers and petitions,
and be merciful, according to our daily needs.

1 Kings 8.57–9*

The Lord is a refuge

The Lord is a refuge for the oppressed,
    a place of safety in times of trouble.
Those who know you, Lord, will trust you;
    you do not abandon anyone who comes to you.

Psalm 9.9–10

All that we desire

You, Lord, give perfect peace
    to those who keep their purpose firm
    and put their trust in you.
We follow your will and put our hope in you;
    You are all that we desire.

Isaiah 26.3,8

Our Lord and Saviour, we thank you

Our Lord and Saviour:
You endured the suffering that should have been ours,
   the pain that we should have borne.

Our Lord and Saviour, we thank you

We are healed by the punishment you suffered,
   made whole by the blows you received.

Our Lord and Saviour, we thank you

You were treated harshly, but endured it humbly;
   you never said a word.

Our Lord and Saviour, we thank you

You were arrested and sentenced and led off to die,
   and no one cared about your fate.

Our Lord and Saviour, we thank you

It was the Father's will that you should suffer;
   your death was a sacrifice to bring forgiveness.

Our Lord and Saviour, we thank you

You willingly gave your life
  and shared the fate of evil men.

Our Lord and Saviour, we thank you

You took the place of many sinners
  and prayed that they might be forgiven.

Our Lord and Saviour, we thank you

Isaiah 53.4,5,7,8,10,12*

Your love

Your love, O God,
  is as powerful as death;
your passion is as strong
  as death itself.
It bursts into flame
  and burns like raging fire.
Water cannot put it out;
  no flood can drown it.

Song of Songs 8.6,7*

Knowing you are near

O Lord our God, we turn to you and pray,
knowing that you are near,
knowing that you are merciful
and quick to forgive.
For your thoughts are not like ours,
and your ways are different from ours.
As high as the heavens are above the earth,
so high are your ways and thoughts above ours.

Isaiah 55.6–9*

FOR ALL THE WORLD

Prayers for justice and peace

Help us to see that justice is done,
and show kindness and mercy
to one another
Zechariah 7.9*

Justice is driven away

Lord, our crimes against you are many.
Our sins accuse us.
We are well aware of them all.
We have rebelled against you, rejected you,
and refused to follow you.
We have oppressed others
and turned away from you.
Our thoughts are false;
our words are lies.
Justice is driven away,
and right cannot come near.
Truth stumbles in the public square,
and honesty finds no place there.
There is so little honesty
    that anyone who stops doing evil
    finds himself the victim of crime.

Isaiah 59.12–15

We look for peace

We look for peace, Lord, but nothing good happens;
   we hope for healing, but terror comes instead.
We have sinned against you, Lord;
   we confess our own sins
   and the sins of our ancestors.

*Jeremiah 14.19,20**

We cry, O Lord, for justice!

Why are you so far away, O Lord?
  Why do you hide yourself when we are in trouble?
The wicked are proud and persecute the poor:
  catch them in the traps they have made.

We cry, O Lord, for justice!

The wicked man is proud of his evil desires;
  the greedy man curses and rejects the Lord.
A wicked man does not care about the Lord;
  in his pride he thinks that God doesn't matter.

We cry, O Lord, for justice!

He hides himself in the villages,
  waiting to murder innocent people.
He spies on his helpless victims;
  he waits in his hiding place like a lion.
He lies in wait for the poor;
  he catches them in his trap and drags them away.

We cry, O Lord, for justice!

The helpless victims lie crushed;
  brute strength has defeated them.
The wicked man says to himself, 'God doesn't care!
  He has closed his eyes and will never see me!'

We cry, O Lord, for justice!

But you do see; you take notice of trouble and suffering
　　and are always ready to help.
The helpless man commits himself to you;
　　you have always helped the needy.

We cry, O Lord, for justice!

Break the power of wicked and evil men;
　　punish them for the wrong they have done
　　until they do it no more.

We cry, O Lord, for justice!

You will listen, O Lord, to the prayers of the lowly;
　　you will give them courage.
You will hear the cries of the oppressed and the orphans;
　　you will judge in their favour,
　　so that mortal men may cause terror no more.

We cry, O Lord, for justice!

Psalm 10.1–4,8–11,14–18*

Wonderful Counsellor

Wonderful Counsellor,
Give us the wisdom of your counsels.

Mighty God,
Show us the glory of your mightiness.

Eternal Father,
Hold us in the arms of your unfailing love.

Prince of Peace,
Unite us in the service of your kingdom.

From now until the end of time.

Isaiah 9.6,7*

Fill us with your spirit

Sovereign Lord,
Fill us with your spirit,
that we may bring good news to the poor
    and heal the broken-hearted;
that we may announce release to the captives
      of injustice and oppression,
    freedom to those in the prison of despair;
that we may proclaim that the time has come
    when you will save your people
      and defeat their enemies;
that we may comfort all who mourn.

Isaiah 61.1,2*

Lead us to the day

Teach us, O Lord, what you want us to do;
    how to walk in the paths you have chosen.
Teach us to hammer our swords into ploughs,
    our spears into pruning-knives.
Lead us to the day when nations will never
      again go to war,
    never again prepare for battle.
Lead us to the day when everyone will
      live in peace
    and no one will make them afraid.

Micah 4.2,3,4*

You have shown us

You have shown us, O Lord, what is good,
what you require of us.
Help us, then, we pray, to do what is just,
and show constant love.
Then we will live, O Lord our God,
in humble fellowship with you.

Micah 6.8*

For all the world

Prepare a banquet, Lord,
for all the world,
a banquet of the richest food
and finest wine.
Remove the cloud of sorrow
that hangs over all the nations.
Destroy death for ever!
Wipe away the tears
and take away the suffering
of the world.
When this happens, we will say,
'You are our God!
We have put our trust in you,
and you have rescued us.
You are the Lord!
We have put our trust in you,
and now we are happy
because you have saved us.'

Isaiah 25.6–9*

The past forgotten

We wait, O Lord, for what you have promised:
a new earth and new heavens,
where the events of the past will be forgotten;
where there will be no weeping,
no calling for help;
where babies will no longer die in infancy,
and all people will live out their life span;
where people will build houses
and live in them themselves –
they will not be used by someone else;
where they will plant vineyards
and enjoy the wine –
it will not be drunk by others;
where they will fully enjoy
the things they have worked for;
where the work they do will be successful,
and their children will not meet with disaster;
where wolves and lambs will eat together;
where lions will eat straw, as cattle do,
and snakes will no longer be dangerous.
We wait, O Lord, for what you have promised.

Isaiah 65.17,19,20,21,22,23,25*

WE HONOUR YOUR NAME

Thanksgiving and praise

Praise the Lord!
His love is eternal!
2 Chronicles 20.21

Your greatness

O Lord, our Lord,
your greatness is seen in all the world!

Your praise reaches up to the heavens;
  it is sung by children and babies.
You are safe and secure from all your enemies;
  you stop anyone who opposes you.

When I look at the sky, which you have made,
  at the moon and the stars, which you set in their places –
what is man, that you think of him;
  mere man, that you care for him?

Yet you made him inferior only to yourself;
  you crowned him with glory and honour.
You appointed him ruler over everything you made;
  you placed him over all creation:
  sheep and cattle, and the wild animals too;
  the birds and the fish
  and the creatures in the seas.

O Lord, our Lord,
  your greatness is seen in all the world!

Psalm 8

May all the peoples praise you!

God, be merciful to us and bless us;
   look on us with kindness,
so that the whole world may know your will;
   so that all nations may know your salvation.

May the peoples praise you, O God;
   may all the peoples praise you!

May the nations be glad and sing for joy,
   because you judge the peoples with justice
   and guide every nation on earth.

May the peoples praise you, O God;
   may all the peoples praise you!

Psalm 67.1–5

We honour your name

O Lord our God, we honour your holy name:
may you be praised for ever and ever!
You are great and powerful,
glorious, splendid and majestic.
Everything in heaven and earth is yours,
and you are king, supreme ruler over all.
All riches and wealth come from you;
you rule everything by your strength and power;
and you are able to make anyone great and strong.
Now, our God, we give you thanks,
and we praise your glorious name.
Yet we cannot really give you anything,
because everything is a gift from you,
and we have only given back what is yours already.
You know, O Lord, that we pass through life
    like exiles and strangers, as our ancestors did.
Our days are like a passing shadow,
and we cannot escape death.
O Lord our God, we honour your holy name.

1 Chronicles 29.10–16*

The Living God

Lord, there is no one like you;
    you are mighty,
    and your name is great and powerful.
Who would not honour you,
    the king of all nations?
Lord, there is no one like you;
    you are the true God,
    you are the living God
    and the eternal king.

Jeremiah 10.6,7,10*

The Lord Almighty

Sovereign Lord,
You made the earth and the sky
by your great power and might;
nothing is too difficult for you.
You are the Lord Almighty.

Jeremiah 32.17,18

Arrow Praises

May the Most High God, who made
heaven and earth, be praised!

Genesis 14.19,20

How great you are, Sovereign Lord!
There is none like you;
we have always known that you alone are God.

2 Samuel 7.22

Praise the Lord God of Israel,
Creator of heaven and earth!

2 Chronicles 2.12

Praise the Lord,
because he is good,
and his love is eternal.

2 Chronicles 5.13

Praise the Lord, the great God!

Nehemiah 8.6

Holy, holy, holy!
The Lord Almighty is holy!
His glory fills the world.

Isaiah 6.3

Give thanks to the Lord Almighty,
because he is good
and his love is eternal.

Jeremiah 33.11

Praise the glory of the Lord in heaven above!

Ezekiel 3.12

OLD TESTAMENT WORDS
FOR CONTEMPLATION

Speak, Lord,
your servant is listening
1 Samuel 3.9

These phrases from the Old Testament – most of them from the book of Isaiah – are for those who wish to include a contemplative element in their prayers. All of them are phrases in which God speaks directly to his people – strengthening, warning, forgiving them. Above all they are expressions of God's inexhaustible love for his creation; a love which seeks a response in the 'prayer of loving regard' which is contemplation.

Anyone who is unfamiliar with this way of praying with the Old Testament may find it helpful to read chapters 3 and 6 of *Contemplating the Word*, a practical handbook by Peter Dodson (SPCK, 1987).

I am who I am.

Exodus 3.14

I am the first, the last, the only God.

Isaiah 44.6

I am the Lord, the Creator of all things.

Isaiah 44.24

I am the high and holy God, who lives
for ever.

Isaiah 57.15

I am merciful.

Jeremiah 3.12

I am everywhere in heaven and on earth.

Jeremiah 23.24

I am the Lord, and I do not change.

Malachi 3.6

I am the Lord your God.

Exodus 20.2

I am the Lord and I make you holy.

Leviticus 22.32

I am the God who forgives your sins.

Isaiah 43.25

I am the Lord who created you.

Isaiah 44.2

I am the one who saves you.

Isaiah 44.22

I am the one who strengthens you.

Isaiah 51.12

I am your father.

Malachi 1.6

Worship no god but me.

Exodus 20.3

Do not abandon me.

Leviticus 19.4

Quietly trust in me.

Isaiah 30.15

Be silent and listen to me.

Isaiah 41.1

You are precious to me.

Isaiah 43.4

You belong to me.

Jeremiah 3.14

Seek me with all your heart.

Jeremiah 29.13

My Spirit is like a fire.

Isaiah 33.11

My victory will endure for all time.

Isaiah 51.8

My love for you will never end.

Isaiah 54.10

My thoughts are not like yours.

Isaiah 55.8

My presence will protect you on
    every side.

Isaiah 58.8

My glory will shine on you.

Isaiah 60.19

My saving power will rise on you
    like the sun.

Malachi 4.2

I . . . have heard your prayer.

Isaiah 38.5

I have called you by name – you are mine.

Isaiah 43.1

I have swept away your sins like a cloud.

Isaiah 44.22

I have written your name on the palms
 of my hands.

Isaiah 49.16

I have given you my power and my teachings.

Isaiah 59.21

I, the Lord, have saved you.

Isaiah 60.16

I have always loved you.

Malachi 1.2

You are stained red with sin, but I
   will wash you as clean as snow.

Isaiah 1.18

Do not be afraid; I will save you.

Isaiah 43.1

When you pass through deep waters,
   I will be with you.

Isaiah 43.2

Even if a mother should forget her child,
   I will never forget you.

Isaiah 49.15

With deep love, I will take you back.

Isaiah 54.7

I turned away angry for only a moment,
   but I will show my love for ever.

Isaiah 54.8

When you pray, I will answer you.

Isaiah 58.9

I will not hold your sins against you.

Isaiah 43.25

I will give you the strength you need.

Isaiah 45.5

I will comfort you . . . as a mother comforts
   her child.

Isaiah 66.13

I will not be angry with you for ever.

Jeremiah 3.12

I will not let you go unpunished.

Jeremiah 30.11

I will sprinkle clean water on you
   and make you clean.

Ezekiel 36.25

I will give you a new heart and a new mind.

Ezekiel 36.26

I will put my Spirit in you.

Ezekiel 36.27

I will save you from everything that
    defiles you.

Ezekiel 36.29

I will be true and faithful.

Hosea 2.19

I will show you constant love and mercy.

Hosea 2.19

I will . . . make you mine for ever.

Hosea 2.19

I will be with you – that is my promise.

Haggai 1.13

I will bless you.

Haggai 2.19

Index of
Biblical References

Praying with
THE NEW TESTAMENT

Compiled by Philip Law
Introduction by Joyce Huggett

Prayers for personal devotion and group worship, using the words of Scripture.

'A fascinating and unusual collection of prayers, skilfully compiled from the words of the Good News version of the New Testament.' *Frank Colquhoun*

'The joy of this compilation of New Testament prayers is that it makes it easy for us to pray God's Word because, under helpful headings, these living words are there, spread before us. As I have attempted to pray these New Testament prayers and to make them my own . . . I have frequently felt like an explorer who has stumbled on an oasis.' *Joyce Huggett*

Praying with
THE JEWISH TRADITION

Translated by Paula Clifford
Introduction by Lionel Blue

Jewish prayers are essentially prayers of a community for that community. And because for the Jew it is quite natural to turn one's thoughts to God at every moment in life, so we find these prayers expressing a wide range of human thoughts and meditations, aspirations, longings and fears, as well as a sense of wonder at the greatness of God and the grandeur of his creation. The prayers in this book have been compiled from a variety of sources, including the Bible, the Talmud and the liturgies of the traditional Jewish festivals. Christians as well as Jews will find much here to enhance their devotional life.

'This book will be most useful where the reader prays and worships. Its spirituality complements but does not contradict a Christian's experience of God, and he or she has the assurance that in some form these prayers were used by Jesus and those who knew him. Even if they seem strange now, they were not strange to the holy family or the apostles.'   *Lionel Blue*